A guide to the care &
feeding of your planet

Earthwise
at play

by Linda Lowery
and
Marybeth Lorbiecki

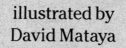

illustrated by
David Mataya

Carolrhoda Books, Inc./Minneapolis

Dear Reader, When you write to organizations listed in this book, please put two first-class stamps inside each envelope to pay for return postage. Also include a note with your name and address on it. Don't worry if it takes four to six weeks for an answer. Remember, too, that if your friends and classmates all write to different organizations, you can share the information you receive (and that saves paper and trees!).

To Hildegard Pesch, who talked with animals, listened to rocks, and left the planet a lovelier place. — LL

To Curt Meine and Nina Leopold Bradley, who opened the door for me to Aldo Leopold; and to Becca, Michael, and Abbie Mataya, who are always opening new doors. — MbL

Special thanks to those individuals and organizations who aided in the research and verification of facts, most especially: Research Biologist Judy Gunkler, Curt Meine of the U.S. National Research Council's Board on Science and Technology for International Development, Cindy Bear, Gail Turner at Environment Canada, Phil Rutter, John Herrington, Kathryn Wild, Beverly Flynn, Cindy Ehrman of the American Minor Breeds Conservancy, Denver Zoo, the Land Institute, Land Stewardship Project, Leopold Center for Sustainable Agriculture, Minnesota Zoological Gardens, National Institute for Urban Wildlife, National Seed Storage Library, National Wildflower Research Center, National Wildlife Federation, and the U.S. Fish and Wildlife Service. Kudos and thanks also to Jean Hagen.

METRIC CONVERSION CHART To find measurements that are almost equal		
WHEN YOU KNOW:	MULTIPLY BY:	TO FIND:
AREA		
acres	0.41	hectares
square miles	2.59	square kilometers
CAPACITY		
gallons	3.79	liters
LENGTH		
feet	30.48	centimeters
yards	0.91	meters
miles	1.61	kilometers
MASS (weight)		
pounds	0.45	kilograms
tons	0.91	metric tons
VOLUME		
cubic yards	0.77	cubic meters
TEMPERATURE degrees Fahrenheit	(subtract 32 and then) 0.56	degrees Celsius

Library of Congress Cataloging-in-Publication Data

Lowery, Linda
  Earthwise at play: a guide to the care & feeding of your planet/ by Linda Lowery and Marybeth Lorbiecki; illustrated by David Mataya.
    p.   cm.
  Includes index.
  Summary: Provides information about various animals and plants and their interdependence, and suggests activities that can help and preserve them.
  ISBN 0-87614-729-5 (lib. bdg.)
  ISBN 0-87614-586-1 (pbk.)
  1. Habitat conservation—Juvenile literature. 2. Nature conservation—Juvenile literature. [1. Conservation of natural resources. 2. Environmental protection. 3. Ecology.]
QH75.L67 1993
639.9'0525—dc20   93-9870
                         CIP
                         AC

Manufactured in the United States of America

1 2 3 4 5 6 98 97 96 95 94 93

This book is available in two editions:
Library binding by
Carolrhoda Books, Inc.
Soft cover by First Avenue Editions
241 First Avenue North
Minneapolis, MN 55401

A teachers' guide is also available through Carolrhoda Books, Inc.

Printed on recycled, recyclable, acid-free paper.

Contents

Photograph Acknowledgments
Front cover: © Arthur Morris/Birds As Art. Back cover:
Independent Picture Service. Georgia Department
of Natural Resources, pp. 3, 39; © Robert Barber, 5;
Independent Picture Service, 6, 30, 37, 44; Jerg Kroener,
9; American Petroleum Institute, 10; © Richard R.
Hewett, 12; Southdale Hennepin Area Library, 13; Kathryn
Wild, 15; Cindy Bear, 16; U.S. Fish and Wildlife Service,
17; 36; Illinois Department of Commerce and Community
Affairs, 18; FAO Photo, 20; Arthur Morris/Birds As Art,
23, 42; World Wildlife Fund, 24; © Alex Kerstitch, 25;
University of Wisconsin Archives c/o Curt Meine, (left)
26; Marybeth Lorbiecki, (right) 26; Ohio DNR, 27;
Colleen Sexton, 31; © Frances M. Roberts, 33, 46;
Library of Congress, 36; USDA Forest Service, 40;
Center for Plant Conservation, 41; Perry J. Reynolds, 43;
Center for Marine Conservation, 45; Kay Shaw, 47.

What Does Earthwise Mean?

Have you heard about the bad things happening to the earth—oil spills, garbage piles, air pollution, poisoned rivers, and things like that? Don't let them get you down. There are things each one of us can do to make the planet healthier. And we can do them wherever we are —in our apartments or houses, our classrooms or schoolyards, our neighborhood parks or county woods.

First we need to find out as much information as we can about how the earth works. Then we will be able to take actions that make sense for the whole planet—actions that are *earthwise*. Sometimes these actions will be fun and easy to do. Sometimes they will be hard. There will even be times when it will be difficult to decide what's the best thing to do. But that's okay. There are always many ways to look at a problem, and it usually takes time to sort out all the facts and possible solutions. We often have to try a few solutions to see which ones work the best.

You can begin your earthwise search here. Your free time is the perfect time to get to know and love your particular place on the planet. Learn how you and your friends can discover the land and wildlife around you. Pick an interesting plant, animal, or wild area, and go for it! Observe, draw, read, talk to experts, and take notes. Become experts yourselves. Don't worry if it takes a while. We have our whole lives to be earthwise explorers.

Make Room for Everyone

The More Kinds the Better

In a box of crayons or markers,
is it better to have just
a few colors, or a lot of them?
A lot of them, of course!
It's best to have a choice
of many shades of red, orange,
yellow, green, blue, and
purple. It's the same with
plants and animals.
There are many kinds, or
species, of plants and animals.
People are a species, and
African elephants are a species.
So are white pines and bluebirds.
Each species has its own way of
eating and living. The more
different species there are
living naturally together in
one place, the healthier
that place is for all.
That's because the
different animals
and plants
help each
other live
and eat.
They don't try to.

It just happens because
they live together.
It's as if you piled all your
friends and family on your bed.
If you moved even one elbow,
you'd make some people
more comfortable
and some more cramped.

APHIDS AND THE FOREST POLICE

Red ants have the nickname "forest police." They eat many insects that harm pine trees while protecting others that are more helpful to the trees. Aphids suck juice from the pine needles and leave behind droppings of a sweet juice called honeydew. This juice is like candy to the ants, so the ants work to keep their candy-makers safe. The trees that have the most honeydew on them attract the most bees. The bees move through the forest, sweeping up pine pollen as they sip. By carrying pollen from tree to tree, they help make new pine cones. Bees, aphids, and red ants—they all keep the forest growing healthily.

FOOD FROM FIGS

For three months a year, the only fruit trees in the Amazon rain forest that produce fruit are fig trees. Toucans, bats, monkeys, and many other animals in the forest live off the figs to keep from starving. And jaguars live off these animals. Even though the toucans, bats, monkeys, and jaguars don't know it, they all depend on one little insect—a wasp! The wasp lays its eggs in figs, and when the baby wasps break out, they carry fig pollen to other fig trees. All 900 kinds of fig trees must be visited by one particular wasp species to make new seeds. If something happens to this wasp, the figs, toucans, bats, monkeys, jaguars, and many other animals in the forest will have nothing to eat.

What one species does affects all the other species in that place. Each species has specific jobs to do to live. With more kinds of species, more jobs get done.

OTTERS AND URCHINS

Sea otters love to eat crabs, and many crab fishers used to hunt otters to save more crabs for themselves. But when the otters disappeared, so did the seals and bald eagles. Why?

Because in some ways, seals and eagles depend on otters. Otters eat sea urchins, which eat sea plants. When the otters disappeared, the sea urchins multiplied. The urchins ate up most of the kelp and sea grass in the area. The fish that live among these plants swam away. Then the seals and eagles, which eat the fish, had to look for new homes too. When the crab fishers stopped hunting the otter, the sea plants grew back. Soon the fish, seals, and eagles returned.

7

To Be or Not to Be

Unfortunately,
many species are in danger.
Over 1,000 animal and plant
species around the world
may soon disappear
from the earth forever.
Once they are gone,
we can't bring them back—
they will be extinct.

Many of the earth's creatures
are already extinct.
There will never be any more
dinosaurs, passenger pigeons,
dodo birds, Carolina parakeets,
or Stellar sea cows.

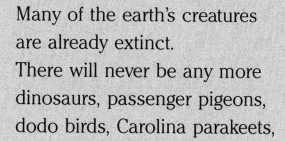

20 OF THE NORTH AMERICAN SPECIES IN DANGER OF EXTINCTION

species	where species is found
Alabama cavefish	AL
American alligator	southeast USA
Carolina northern flying squirrel	NC, TN
Delta green ground beetle	CA
Desert tortoise	southwest USA, Mexico
Florida panther	southeast USA
Giant kangaroo rat	USA
Gila trout	AZ, NM
Gray wolf	Canada, USA, Mexico
Grizzly bear	northwest USA
Hawaiian monk seal	HI
Minnesota trout lily	MN
Mountain sweet pitcher plant	NC, SC
Orange-footed pearly mussel	USA
Oregon silver spot butterfly	OR, WA
Ozark big-eared bat	MO, OK, AR
Piping plover	throughout North America
St. Thomas prickly ash	Puerto Rico, Virgin Islands
Whooping crane	throughout North America
Wood bison	Canada, northwest USA

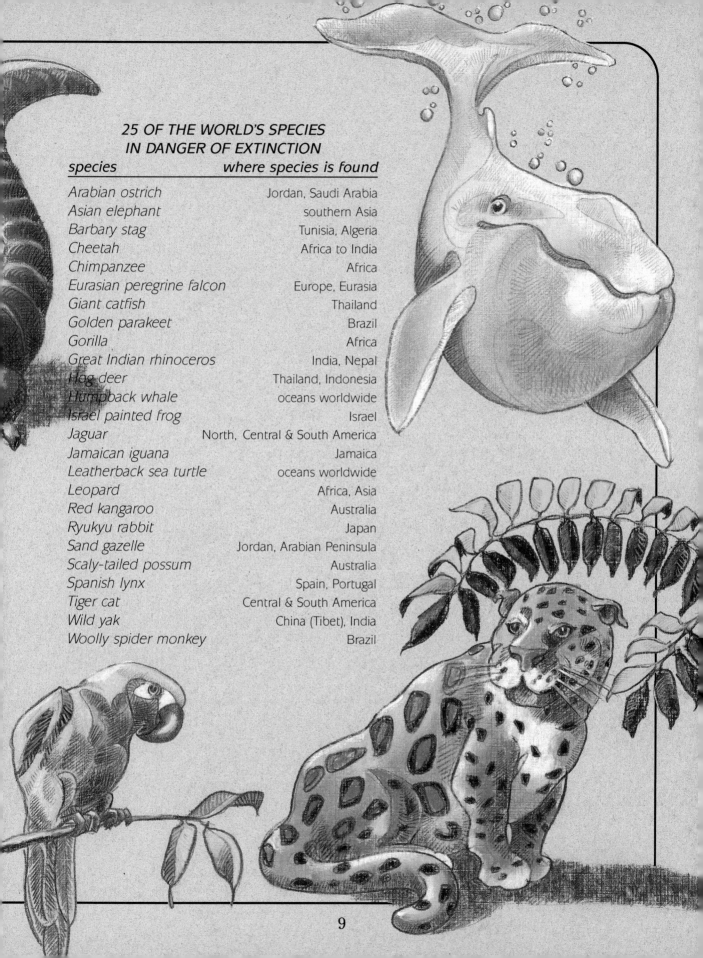

25 OF THE WORLD'S SPECIES IN DANGER OF EXTINCTION

species	where species is found
Arabian ostrich	Jordan, Saudi Arabia
Asian elephant	southern Asia
Barbary stag	Tunisia, Algeria
Cheetah	Africa to India
Chimpanzee	Africa
Eurasian peregrine falcon	Europe, Eurasia
Giant catfish	Thailand
Golden parakeet	Brazil
Gorilla	Africa
Great Indian rhinoceros	India, Nepal
Hog deer	Thailand, Indonesia
Humpback whale	oceans worldwide
Israel painted frog	Israel
Jaguar	North, Central & South America
Jamaican iguana	Jamaica
Leatherback sea turtle	oceans worldwide
Leopard	Africa, Asia
Red kangaroo	Australia
Ryukyu rabbit	Japan
Sand gazelle	Jordan, Arabian Peninsula
Scaly-tailed possum	Australia
Spanish lynx	Spain, Portugal
Tiger cat	Central & South America
Wild yak	China (Tibet), India
Woolly spider monkey	Brazil

What's the Problem?

A species can become extinct
for many reasons.
The climate may change,
a disaster may happen,
or one species may beat out
another species for food.
Lately, though, people are
causing many animals and
plants to become extinct.
Pollution makes it hard
for wild species to find
safe food and water.
Building, mining, logging,
farming, oil drilling, and tourists
are taking away their homes.

Certain wild species
are being shot, trapped,
fished, cut, or picked
faster than they can grow
and have young.
Some scientists think that
at least 74 species
become extinct each day.
That is 1,000 to 10,000
times more than in
any other time period
in human history.
Yet things are not hopeless.
If people decide to live
in a more earthwise way,
there can be food, water,
and room for us all.

THE GREEN GIANT OF THE SEA

In the Caribbean, a streak of green flashes through turquoise waters. What can it be? It's a 400-pound green sea turtle. These mammoth turtles can swim as fast as 20 miles per hour. Like other turtles around the world, though, green sea turtles are having troubles. The beaches where they lay their eggs are filling up with buildings and tourists. Plus, many people think the sea turtles are quite tasty, so the turtles are being hunted down to be served in restaurants.

A DEADLY TOOTHACHE

Q: What is gray, weighs 16,000 pounds, and can drink 50 gallons of water in one day?
A: An elephant. The African elephant is the largest animal on land. By the time you are 25 years old, African elephants might be gone from the earth forever.

Why? Because their enormous tusks are made of ivory, and people make boxes, jewelry, piano keys, and other beautiful things out of ivory. To get the ivory, people kill elephants.

A DYING COMMUNITY

The Yanomami people live in the Amazon rain forest of Brazil. The rain forest is being burned and cut down for timber, ranches, and farms. So the Yanomami have fewer places to live and hunt. They have also gotten sick from illnesses carried by the new strangers in the forest. The Yanomami are worried about what they must do to stay alive.

MORE COATS MEAN FEWER LEOPARDS

Snow leopards live high in the mountains of Asia. In summer, their fur is silver and black. In winter, it turns white like the snow. Leopards are being killed to make coats out of their beautiful fur, and now there are fewer than 500 snow leopards left in the world.

CANADA'S SECRETIVE SEABIRD

The marbled murrelet is a small bird that nests in the tops of tall, old trees. These trees make up the ancient forests along the North Pacific Ocean.

Bird-watchers have been trying to spot a marbled murrelet nest in Canada for 100 years. Finally, in August 1990, one nest was found. But this nest may not last long. Loggers in British Columbia are quickly cutting the ancient forests down. The marbled murrelet will be in danger if these old forests are not protected.

A TREE THAT SAW THE DINOSAURS

Not a lot of creatures living today were around during the time of dinosaurs. But the stinking cedar was. It has existed for more than 100 million years. It lives in the swamps of Florida and southern Georgia. These days, though, stinking cedars are having health problems. Pollution has made many of the trees sick. Other cedars have been killed by diseases brought by trees planted after logging. If these health problems go on, they could put an end to the stinking cedar's long history.

SAD SALMON

In the summer and fall, five species of ocean salmon swim up streams along the northern Pacific coast to lay their eggs. The fish have to come back to the exact stream bed where they were hatched. Some salmon must travel as far as 800 miles upstream. It's a long and tiring trip.

Dams, river pollution, and predators are killing the salmon before they can lay their eggs. Dams hold back the streams' waters. Sea lions wait at the dams' fish ladders to scoop up the salmon. Then if the salmon manage to swim past the dangers to lay their eggs, many of the little hatched salmon get chewed up by the dam on their way to the ocean.

BEING A PICKY EATER CAN BE DANGEROUS

Koalas live in Australia, and they eat the leaves of only one kind of tree—the eucalyptus tree. Each week, whole forests of eucalyptus trees are being cut to make farms and build factories. The koalas are left with no food to eat. One by one, koalas are disappearing from Australia.

HOME WANTED: A MEADOW WILL DO

All over the U.S. and Canada, fields, meadows, and vacant lots are being paved for parking lots. So where's a butterfly to go for a nice place to live? Many butterflies are left without homes when wild grasses and flowers are removed to pave over the land.

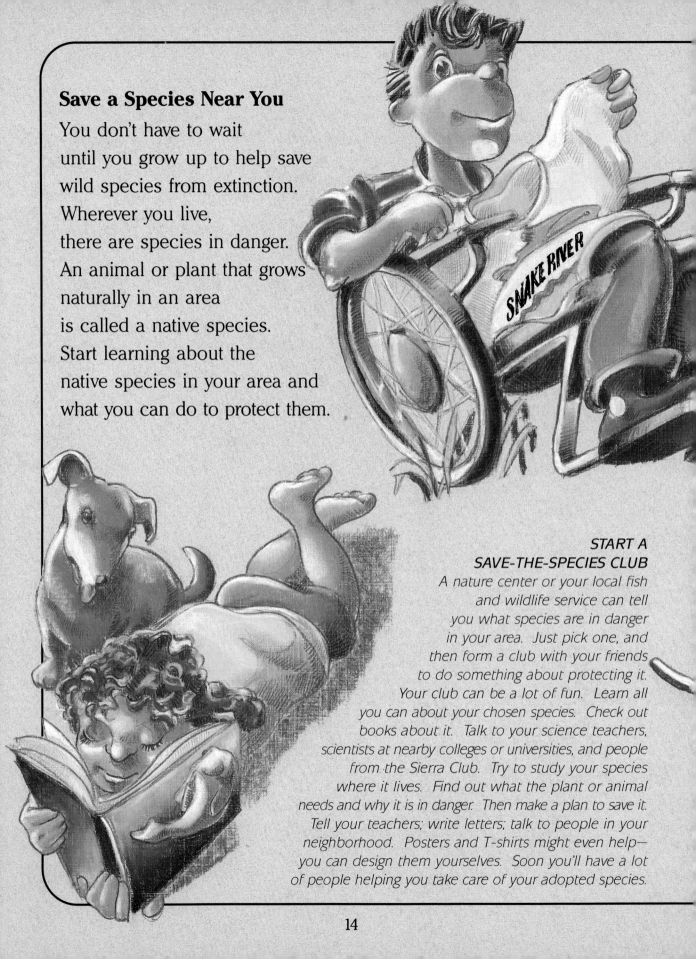

Save a Species Near You

You don't have to wait
until you grow up to help save
wild species from extinction.
Wherever you live,
there are species in danger.
An animal or plant that grows
naturally in an area
is called a native species.
Start learning about the
native species in your area and
what you can do to protect them.

START A
SAVE-THE-SPECIES CLUB

*A nature center or your local fish
and wildlife service can tell
you what species are in danger
in your area. Just pick one, and
then form a club with your friends
to do something about protecting it.
Your club can be a lot of fun. Learn all
you can about your chosen species. Check out
books about it. Talk to your science teachers,
scientists at nearby colleges or universities, and people
from the Sierra Club. Try to study your species
where it lives. Find out what the plant or animal
needs and why it is in danger. Then make a plan to save it.
Tell your teachers; write letters; talk to people in your
neighborhood. Posters and T-shirts might even help—
you can design them yourselves. Soon you'll have a lot
of people helping you take care of your adopted species.*

HOW TO SAVE A MINT

In San Diego, California, a first-grader at the Albert Joe Hickman Elementary School wanted to start an ecology club. With Kathryn Wild's help, the club got organized and adopted a neighborhood plant—the San Diego Mesa mint. This plant grows in only two places in the world. Yet a company wanted to build houses in one of these areas.

The children alerted the California Department of Fish and Game that the plant was in danger and needed protection. Through letters to the newspaper, neighborhood meetings, posters, and door-to-door visits, the kids let everyone in the city know the mint was in trouble. Kids from other schools, neighbors, and local businesses helped save the mint's habitat.

Now ecology clubs are starting in schools all over San Diego. Each club is picking a species to study and protect. The state of California has asked the Hickman Elementary club to be a model for all schools in the state.

Jenny Coulter (left) and Lani Wild (right) at the vernal pools they helped save. Vernal pools are the habitat of the San Diego mesa mint. Lani's idea to start the "Children's Ecology Club" has grown to include three schools and over 75 members.

NATURE CENTERS NEED YOU

Most counties and cities have nature centers and parks. These places often need volunteers to plant trees, clean up litter, make homes for birds or animals, or study species. Why don't you and your family or friends volunteer? Think how much fun you can have while you're helping protect your neighborhood species.

15

CHEERS FOR CHESTNUTS!

"Chestnuts roasting on an open fire…" Some people fear that this scene from the holiday song may someday be only a memory. Most American chestnut trees have been killed by a tree disease brought in from China. But some people are working to bring back the chestnut trees before it's too late. They would love to have your help! Write to:

The American Chestnut Foundation
401 Brooks Hall—WVU
P.O. Box 6057
Morgantown, WV 26506-6057

SCHOOLYARD SCIENTISTS

To help wildlife scientists learn more about burrowing owls, elementary schoolchildren in Fort Myers, Florida, built owl perches in their playground. At certain times each day, they watched the owls and took careful notes on their actions. The students' notes became part of the University of Florida's study project on the lives of burrowing owls. Now kids at other Florida schools are starting wildlife research projects too. Maybe there are researchers at a university or wildlife center near you who could use your help.

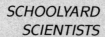

A HOWLIN' GOOD TIME

In the 1830s, about 25,000 wolves lived in Wisconsin. They helped keep deer herds from growing too big. If a deer herd gets too large, it eats up all the small, new trees in the forest.

Unfortunately, most people at that time didn't understand how important wolves are for keeping the forests and deer healthy. They thought hunters could do the same job wolves can. Also, they were afraid of the animals. By 1960, every wolf in the state had been shot, poisoned, or run into Canada. The deer herds grew so large that the forests had trouble growing, and many deer starved to death.

Some people wanted to bring back the wolves. Kids in northern Wisconsin offered their help. They adopted wolves through the state's Adopt-A-Wolf program. With their teachers and parents, the children worked to teach the people of Wisconsin about wolves so they wouldn't be afraid of them. Slowly, wolves are returning to Wisconsin. Now many other states are putting together programs like this. Look for one in your area.

OSPREY, COME HOME

Thousands of large, fish-eating birds called ospreys used to live around the Chesapeake Bay. Then the farm chemical DDT started to wash into the bay from nearby fields. The DDT poisoned the fish the birds ate. Female ospreys that ate the poisoned fish laid eggs with weak shells. The eggshells crumbled before the young ospreys could hatch. Finally a bill was passed that outlawed DDT. But then the problem was that the ospreys no longer had places to nest. Many of the tall trees along the bay's shore had been cut down. The people who lived around the bay decided to do something to bring the big birds back. They sank tall poles with platforms on top into the bay. The ospreys flew to these perches and built their nests there. Now residents along the Chesapeake Bay are watching their beloved ospreys return each spring to nest and spend the summer.

Make Faraway Friends

Many species around the world need to be protected to survive. Just as you can have a pen pal in a faraway place, you can also build a special friendship with an animal from another part of the world. Visit zoos, watch nature programs, and read about other countries. Pick a favorite species and learn as much as possible about it. Soon you'll discover ways you can help protect it.

PLEASE DO NOT FEED THE ANIMALS

Zookeepers feed the animals just the right food to keep them healthy. Some people, though, like to give the animals a taste of human food. This is very dangerous for the animals. So instead of feeding them, why not stop by at feeding time and see what the zookeepers give them? This will help you learn what these animals eat in the wild. Which animals eat only fruits and leaves? Which eat fish? Which animals like raw meat?

HOW DO YOU ZOO?

More and more these days, zoos are helping save wild animals from becoming extinct. The zoos give mammals, birds, fish, and reptiles safe places to live until they can be protected in their wild habitats. The California condor was saved by zoos. So were the American bison, the Siberian tiger, and the Arabian oryx. Zoos are now working hard to save the giant panda, the snow leopard, and others. Whenever they can, zoos put some of these animals back into the wild places where they belong.

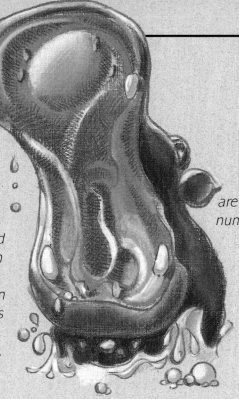

ZOO ADOPTION

Imagine how much it costs to feed a hippo! You and your family can help a zoo take care of your favorite animal by paying a certain amount each year. (The amount is decided by the zoo.) You will receive a photo, adoption papers, and a letter telling you how your animal is doing. Ask about adoption at the information desk next time you visit the zoo.

SIGNS OF THE TIMES

The animals that are most in danger of becoming extinct are called endangered animals. This means that only small numbers of these animals are left in the world, and the numbers are growing smaller. Other species in trouble are called threatened species. This means that if things don't change right away, these species will become endangered. At the zoo, you will see a sign like this for all endangered and threatened animals:

If the zoo is working with scientists to help save an endangered or threatened species, you will see a sign that looks like this:

Species Survival Plan

WILD ORPHANS

What happens to baby elephants whose parents were killed for ivory? They can't survive by themselves. When people find these elephants, they bring them to an animal orphanage in Kenya, Africa. These baby elephants and other wild baby animals are cared for there until they are old enough to live on their own in the wild.

Many North American counties and cities have wild-life orphanages and care centers too. Call your zoo to find out if there's one near you.

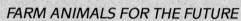

Put a Little Variety in Your Life

Just as there are many different races of people in the world, there are often many races, or varieties, of species. The more varieties there are of a species, the less likely it is that the species will become extinct. Yet many varieties of species are dying out too.

FARM ANIMALS FOR THE FUTURE

At one time, there were many varieties of turkeys, pigs, cows, chickens, goats, and horses. Now almost ½ of them are extinct or nearly so. Only a very few varieties of these animals are being raised on farms today.

Just like Noah and his ark, some farmers are trying to save old-time farm animals for the future. Some of these animals, such as Dutch belted oxen, Scotch Highland cattle, or Tamworth pigs, can be seen at the Plimouth Plantation in Virginia. For information about saving old-time farm animals, write to: American Minor Breeds Conservancy P.O. Box 477 Pittsboro, NC 27312

GREEN EGGS AND HAM?

Did you know that when you eat eggs with green, blue, or brown shells, you are helping save rare chickens? These eggs taste the same as eggs with white shells, but they are from different varieties of chickens. The more you eat these unusual kinds of eggs, the more farmers will raise rare varieties of chickens.

SAVE THAT SEED!

In 1970 nearly all the corn planted in the U.S. was of a similar variety. Then a corn disease wiped out ½ the nation's crop. Could it have been stopped?

Yes!—if farmers had been growing many different varieties of corn. But many old-time kinds of corn and other farm plants are hard to find now. For example, over 7,000 varieties of apple trees were grown in North America a hundred years ago.

Now only 500 to 600 exist. Many people are working to save old-time plants by growing them and storing their seeds. To buy a kit for growing old-time vegetables, write to:

Minnesota Historical Society
Oliver H. Kelley Farm
15788 Kelley Farm Road
Elk River, MN 55330

A GROWING LIBRARY

Where can researchers check out seeds rather than books? At the National Seed Storage Library in Fort Collins, Colorado. If you're in the area, you're welcome to take a tour!

SEED SCOUTS

Because seeds are so important, plant hunters travel around the world looking for rare crops, such as pink potatoes, purple-skinned peanuts, and white sunflowers. These plants might just be the plants farmers will need in the future. A group from Arizona, called Native Seed/SEARCH, sends hunters to the highlands of Peru, the rain forests of Ecuador, the fields of Turkey, and many other faraway places.

CAREFUL COLLECTORS

Q: Where can you find the largest collection of barley and oat seeds in the world?
A: Canada.

In addition, the largest collection of rice seeds is stored in the Philippines, and the Seed Savers' Exchange in Decorah, Iowa, has over 5,000 kinds of seeds from around the world.

Home Sweet Habitat

Where's a Creature to Live?

Everyone has to live somewhere.
Ducks need lakes, rivers,
and marshes.
Butterflies need meadows
filled with wildflowers.
Cacti need deserts.
Each place—lake, river, marsh,
prairie, desert, forest, ocean,
tundra, farm, and city—
is called a "habitat."
A habitat is a home—
the place where a species
        lives naturally.
            Billions of
            different beings
            live together
            in a habitat.
            Some beings
            are so tiny
            you can't
            see them
            without a
            microscope.

Others are huge,
like moose or whales.
All have a part in making a
habitat a healthy place to live.
Protecting habitats is
just as important as
protecting species and varieties.
After all, where's a creature to live
        if its habitat disappears?

WHAT'S IN A WETLAND?

Some people think that marshes, swamps, and bogs aren't worth very much. But these wetlands are the habitat for many species.

Algae, marsh reeds, and water lilies use energy from the sun, minerals from the mud, and water to make food for themselves. As the plants suck up the water, they clean it before it seeps deep into the earth. Moose and ducks feed off the algae, the marsh plants, and the flowers. Waterbugs swim in and out of the reeds, and bees drink up the sweet juices in the flowers. Birds and reptiles feast off the insects. Guess who shows up then?

Hawks and wolves (and people too). They hunt the birds and the animals. They leave droppings and bones that become part of the marsh's nutrients.

Ponds, estuaries, river bottomlands, and bayous are all wetlands too. Wetlands in North America are being drained for building or farming, or they are being polluted by oil drilling and farm chemicals. You can help save wetlands by learning more about them and letting people know how important they are. Visit a wetland near you to see how many different species you can find living there.

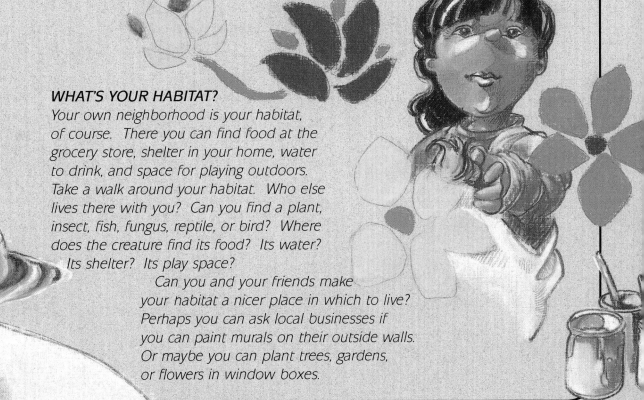

WHAT'S YOUR HABITAT?

Your own neighborhood is your habitat, of course. There you can find food at the grocery store, shelter in your home, water to drink, and space for playing outdoors. Take a walk around your habitat. Who else lives there with you? Can you find a plant, insect, fish, fungus, reptile, or bird? Where does the creature find its food? Its water? Its shelter? Its play space?

Can you and your friends make your habitat a nicer place in which to live? Perhaps you can ask local businesses if you can paint murals on their outside walls. Or maybe you can plant trees, gardens, or flowers in window boxes.

A SPECIES STOREHOUSE

Did you know that more species of ants live in one tree in Peru than in all of England?

Peru has rain forests, and rain forests are filled to the treetops with many different species. In fact, more species live in rain forests near the equator than any other place in the world. For example, scientists have counted about 543 species of butterflies, 850 species of birds, 150 species of reptiles living in tropical rain forests. There may be 10 to 30 million species of insects. There are so many species living in these forests that scientists haven't even discovered them all yet.

Each year, however, an average of 50 million acres of rain forest (or 100 acres per minute) are burned to make farms or cut down for timber. That's about the size of England, Wales, and Scotland put together.

A lot of people are trying to stop this destruction. You and your family can help too. Write to:

Rainforest Action Network
450 Sansome St., Suite 700
San Francisco, CA 94111

Rainforest Alliance
270 Lafayette St., Suite 512
New York, NY 10012

VACATIONING IN THE RAIN FOREST

Many of North America's prettiest species—its brightly colored songbirds and butterflies—spend their winters in the rain forests near the equator. Each spring, they fly thousands of miles to live and lay eggs in our woods, prairies, deserts, beaches, and wetlands. As the rain forests are cut or burned, we are seeing fewer of these beautiful summer visitors.

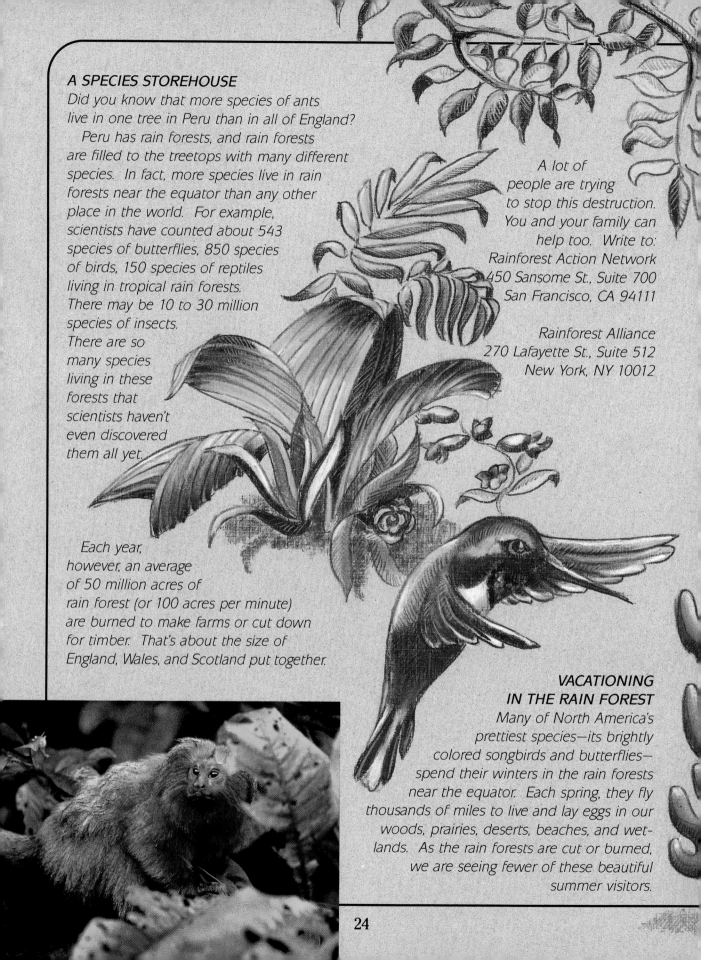

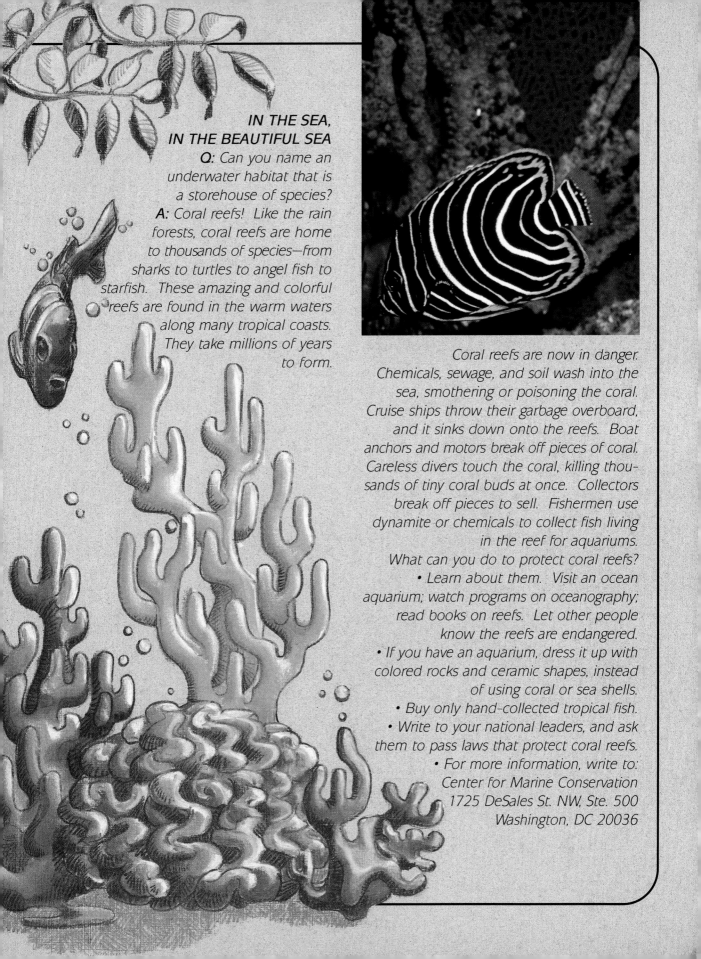

IN THE SEA,
IN THE BEAUTIFUL SEA

Q: Can you name an underwater habitat that is a storehouse of species?
A: Coral reefs! Like the rain forests, coral reefs are home to thousands of species—from sharks to turtles to angel fish to starfish. These amazing and colorful reefs are found in the warm waters along many tropical coasts. They take millions of years to form.

Coral reefs are now in danger. Chemicals, sewage, and soil wash into the sea, smothering or poisoning the coral. Cruise ships throw their garbage overboard, and it sinks down onto the reefs. Boat anchors and motors break off pieces of coral. Careless divers touch the coral, killing thousands of tiny coral buds at once. Collectors break off pieces to sell. Fishermen use dynamite or chemicals to collect fish living in the reef for aquariums.

What can you do to protect coral reefs?

• Learn about them. Visit an ocean aquarium; watch programs on oceanography; read books on reefs. Let other people know the reefs are endangered.

• If you have an aquarium, dress it up with colored rocks and ceramic shapes, instead of using coral or sea shells.

• Buy only hand-collected tropical fish.

• Write to your national leaders, and ask them to pass laws that protect coral reefs.

• For more information, write to: Center for Marine Conservation 1725 DeSales St. NW, Ste. 500 Washington, DC 20036

Bringing Back Habitats

When forests have been cut down,
grasslands have been plowed over,
and wetlands have been drained,
can these habitats ever be healthy
and full of life again?
The good news is that
yes, sometimes they can.
It takes a lot of hard work, time,
and people with creative ideas.

Within ten years, the many different trees, grasses, and flowers were growing on their own. Wild birds and animals had moved in to live. The land was no longer a sandy wasteland—it was a woods next to a prairie next to a marsh.

Mr. Leopold taught many people how to care for the land. He wrote, "When we see land as a community to which we belong, we may begin to use it with love and respect."

SAND COUNTY TURNAROUND

In 1935, Aldo Leopold bought some land that had been ruined by bad farming. The place had only an old chicken coop, a few trees, and many acres of sand.

Mr. Leopold and his family wanted to make the land healthy again. So each spring, they planted thousands of trees. Throughout the summer, they used buckets to bring them water. They also planted prairie grasses and native wildflowers.

26

OASIS IN A DRY LAND

In Kenya, a cement company had stripped the top layers of soil and limestone off 900 acres, leaving them a lifeless wasteland. Yet Rene Haller, a Swiss scientist, turned over 250 acres into a lush place, filled with trees, grasses, insects, reptiles, birds, and animals.

To start, Dr. Haller dug into the limestone to plant hardy, fast-growing trees and grasses. After a layer of dead leaves piled up, he added millipedes. These insects helped turn the leaves into soil. Then Dr. Haller brought in some native animals, such as desert sheep, goats, antelope, and oryx. The animals ate the leaves and grasses, and left manure. Then lions moved in and kept the animals from becoming too numerous. Dr. Haller also started fish ponds, which attracted insects and birds.

Soon the land began to heal. Suddenly the local people could hunt and fish and have jobs working to restore the land. "It's surprising what nature can do when you lend a helping hand," said Dr. Haller.

STREAMS NEED SAVING TOO

Streams are habitats for fish, reptiles, insects, birds, and animals. But many streams, rivers, and creeks have become muddy and polluted. Kids can help make these waters sparkling clear again by planting rows of trees along the banks to hold back the soil, by picking up litter, and by urging the community to take care of its waters.

The Girls Club of Wilmington, Delaware, helped clean up the Little Mill Creek, and now they are helping it stay that way. They are testing the river for stone fly nymphs. If the nymphs are buzzing around, that means the water is clean. The girls send their findings to Save Our Streams. This group keeps track of the results and sends them to government pollution-control agencies. To clean up and test waters near you, write to:

Save Our Streams
Izaak Walton League
1401 Wilson Boulevard
Arlington, VA 22209

Adopt-A-Stream
Foundation
P.O. Box 55588
Everett, WA 98206

Backyard Welcome

Wherever you live,
you can track down a place
to make a habitat for wildlife.
If you live in an apartment,
ask the owner or manager
about using a back or side yard.
Talk to other kids in your building
to see if they want to help.
There might also be a space
at school to use.
You can even talk to people from
your local park or city council.
They may know of a vacant lot
you can transform
into a wildlife park.
If you live in a house,
your backyard
may be the perfect spot.
Just remember that
animals need the same things
people do: food, water, homes,
and places to run and hide.

You can make your place inviting
with trees, flowers, and bushes;
birdbaths, feeders, and houses;
old logs, sand piles, and ponds.
For directions and more ideas,
go to the library or write to:

National Wildlife Federation
Backyard Habitat Program
1400 16th Street NW
Washington, DC 20036-2266
(Their Backyard Information
Packet # 79919 costs less
than a ticket to most movies.)

EVERYONE'S PARK
In Marietta, Georgia,
students, teachers, parents,
and friends turned 5½ acres
of dirt behind a school into
a safe place for wildlife.
They planted trees, grasses, and
wildflowers. They left overgrown
shrubs and rotting logs where
they found them. They dug ponds
and made a trail through a
bog. Now the whole school
and city can use this park to
watch and study the wildlife
that live there.

ROOFTOP RETREATS

Q: What do you do when you are surrounded by buildings?

A: Plant on the roof! Some building owners are hauling in topsoil, grasses, wildflowers, trees, and bushes to make their flat rooftops into gardens and parks. These lovely spots give migrating birds and butterflies spaces to rest and eat. And they make the city a more beautiful and healthy place to live.

HOMES AND HIDEOUTS

Q: Where do wild animals and birds go to hide, nest, and look for food?

A: In rotting logs and trees, brush piles and grape tangles, grassy ditches and weeds along fences. If you want wildlife to live near you, you need to build these small habitats or avoid cleaning up the ones nature builds. Many farmers leave places of cover on their lands, and so can you. Watch how many different animals gather there.

MAKING A SPLASH OF IT

Mud puddles, birdbaths, and miniponds are favorites for wildlife who want to swim, sip, or splash. You can make one yourself by scooping a hole in the dirt and laying an old plastic garbage-can lid in it upside down. Place your lid under a sturdy tree branch or clothesline (at least 15 feet away from bushes, where cats can hide). Fill the lid with water. Then put a few tiny holes in the bottom of an old bucket. Hang the bucket from the branch or clothesline. Fill the bucket with water, and let it drip. Now you've got a natural shower for wildlife. (Don't forget to fill the bucket when it's empty!)

If you dig a bigger hole and line it with plastic sheeting, you can add algae, frogs, turtles, and maybe even a water lily. Then you'll have your own frog pond to watch.

A PAGE FROM NATURE

Q: Where can you read news about wildlife and habitats?
A: In magazines written especially for kids who love nature. Here are some:

Owl *(ages 9-12)*
Chickadee *(ages 3-6)*
255 Great Arrow Avenue
Buffalo, NY 14207-3082

Ranger Rick *(ages 7-12)*
Your Big Backyard *(ages 3-5)*
National Wildlife Federation
1400 16th Street NW
Washington, DC 20036-2266

Zoo Books *(ages 4-10)*
P.O. Box 85271
San Diego, CA 92138

HIGHWAY HAVENS

Crisscrossing North America are roads, roads, and more roads. The land along these roads can be made into beautiful wildlife habitats. People are placing bird-houses on the backs of signs and billboards. They're planting native trees, grasses, and wildflowers along the shoulders. They're leaving drainage ditches swampy for wild ducks, geese, cranes, and other birds.

Call your local highway department to see if you, your friends, and your family can Adopt-A-Mile of roadway to make into a habitat. For more information on roadsides for wildlife, write to:

Department of Natural Resources
Roadside Specialist
Box 756, Highway 15 South
New Ulm, MN 56073

HABITAT FOR HUMANITY

Former President Jimmy Carter thought homeless families needed good habitats too. So he and his wife, Rosalynn, started a group to help make homes for people who can't afford them. One family helps another family build a house. Then the first family gets help back. For more information, call the Habitat for Humanity organization near you.

PET PREDATORS

Cats and dogs kill thousands of songbirds and small wildlife each year. When only 1 pet cat in 10 in North America kills a bird a day, 4.4 million birds die daily. You can help protect wildlife by putting bells on your pets' collars or watching your animals if you let them roam outdoors.

City Livin'

As we build more and more homes, hotels, factories, and stores, wild plants and animals are left homeless. People who plan cities are trying to find ways to build and expand cities so they make good habitats for people *and* wildlife.

ECO-CITY

Q: Where can you find bike lanes, sidewalks, hiking trails, and wildlife paths all in the same city?

A: Cierro Gordo, in Oregon. This is a model environmental city. The city center, shops, post offices, and restaurants are all within walking distance. There are large parks, woods, and meadows. Wide strips of land that go from one side of the city to the other have been left untouched so wildlife can travel right through town without being hit by cars. Recycling, composting, solar energy, and other earthwise ways of living are part of the city's plan.

NATURAL DESIGNS

How do builders, architects, city planners, businesses, and organizations know how to plan for wildlife? They talk to environmental planners! These professionals help people and wildlife live together in the same habitat. Two groups in Maryland—the National Institute for Urban Wildlife, in Columbia, and the Natural Design and Development Project, in Annapolis—also give people advice on how to make their city spaces more inviting to wildlife. Some cities and neighborhoods don't have environmental planners. People in these places often work with public health nurses to make their habitats healthier for all species. For more information, write to:

Dr. Beverly Flynn
Healthy Cities Indiana
Indiana University
1111 Middle Drive, NU 237
Indianapolis, IN 46202

TURNING A CITY GREEN

Kids in cities and towns throughout Canada and the U.S. are helping to make their habitats green. For example, in New York City, children helped plant gardens in vacant lots between apartment buildings. In Los Angeles, they planted thousands of trees with an organization called TreePeople.

You can do it too! Call your neighborhood or city council, and see if they know of a green project in your area. Or get together with some friends to start your own. The book The Simple Act of Planting a Tree by Jeremy P. Tarcher, will tell you how. Here's a group that has helped over 1.2 million kids plant trees in their areas:

Trees for Life
1103 Jefferson
Wichita, KS 67203

NEIGHBORHOOD NATURE

You can be an environmental planner for your neighborhood. Get out some colored pencils and paper. Now use your imagination on your own neighborhood! How can you make it a better place for wildlife? Make a vacant lot into a park? Plant trees and bushes near the highways and roads? Mark streets with safe biking lanes? Put window boxes with plants on all the shops? Hang planters from clotheslines strung between buildings? Go wild! Make pictures, maps, and plans, and send them to your city council.

Down on the Farm

Because farmers work
on large plots of land,
they are some of the most
important people in helping to
save animals, plants, and habitats.
But it isn't always easy.
It takes time to come up
with ways to farm that are good
for everyone—the farmers,
the farmland and farm animals,
the people who eat the food,
and the local wildlife.
Like other scientists,
earthwise farmers are constantly
experimenting—finding ways
to farm better and make
their farm habitats healthier.

TOUGH TIMES AND SUSTAINABLE SOLUTIONS

It is expensive to run a farm. To make ends meet, farmers often use farming methods that harm the land and animals. They plow fields so large that the topsoil is left unprotected. It gets blown or washed away. They put tons of chemicals on their fields to keep away pests and make crops grow better. The chemicals poison the soil, water, food, and wildlife (and sometimes the farmers). They keep the farm animals in small pens or cages, and they also give the animals shots to make them grow bigger. The shots can be bad for the animals and for the people who eat the food later.

Poor farming and a lack of rain in the 1930s created the "Dust Bowl" in the American South and Midwest. The topsoil turned to dust and blew across the continent in enormous storms. Many acres of land turned into desert.

TOPSOIL TURMOIL

Topsoil is the earth's rich, dark, top layer of dirt, and it is the best soil for raising plants. Topsoil takes a long time to make. It is made by different species of plants and animals living together on a piece of ground. One plant puts a nutrient in the soil; the plant next to it puts a different one in. Dead leaves and animals, decaying vegetables, and animal droppings pile up on top of the ground, adding other nutrients. Insects, fungi, earthworms, lichen, snails, slugs, and microorganisms in the soil break up the nutrients and spread them around. The roots of grasses, wildflowers, bushes, and trees hold the topsoil in place.

What happens when the land is plowed, bulldozed, or cleared of trees? Then there is nothing to hold the topsoil down, so wind blows it away. Or rain washes the topsoil into rivers, lakes, wetlands, and oceans. Each year, thousands of tons of topsoil are lost. In Iowa, two bushels of topsoil are lost for every bushel of corn grown. Around the world, lands are losing their topsoil and plants. Farmlands are drying into deserts, and people are starving.

To learn how to save our topsoil, call 1-800-THE-SOIL and ask for a kid's information packet.

Many farmers are experimenting with ways to farm that are healthier for all species (and may even cost less). These farmers plant smaller fields with trees around them so the seeds and topsoil won't blow away. They grow two or three crops in the same field in different rows. This keeps the soil more nutritious and makes it harder for pesty insects to invade. The farmers change crops every year to give the soil a rest. They use compost and manure instead of chemical fertilizers. They plant species that are hardy against pests and dryness. They let their animals graze in open fields, and they move the animals often so the land doesn't get worn out. They also leave marshes, swamps, rotting logs, and brush piles for wildlife.

These methods are called "sustainable farming."
For more information, write to:

The Land Stewardship Project
14758 Ostlund Trail North
Marine, MN 55047

PRAIRIE POWER

Q: How long does it take a prairie to make one inch of new topsoil?
- a) 1 year
- b) 10 years
- c) 100 years

A: c) 100 years! Prairies make some of the best soil in the world. Prairies are also important habitats for plants, birds, animals, and insects.

The central part of North America was once covered with prairies of tall grasses and wildflowers. But most of America's prairies were plowed under for farming. Now people in Canada and the U.S. are trying to save prairies or to replant them. Many of these prairies are in parks that welcome visitors.

FOOD FROM THE PRAIRIE

Have you ever eaten a prairie-grass muffin? Maybe you will someday soon. Like the early Native Americans, farmers at the Land Institute in Salina, Kansas, are using prairie plants for food. The seeds from these grasses can be used to make flour, just as wheat seeds can. The difference is that these grasses come up year after year without being replanted. They are strong enough to survive most insects, wind, drought, or frost. Their roots hold down the soil and even help make new soil. So if you're ever in Salina, visit the institute and see what the future of farming might look like.

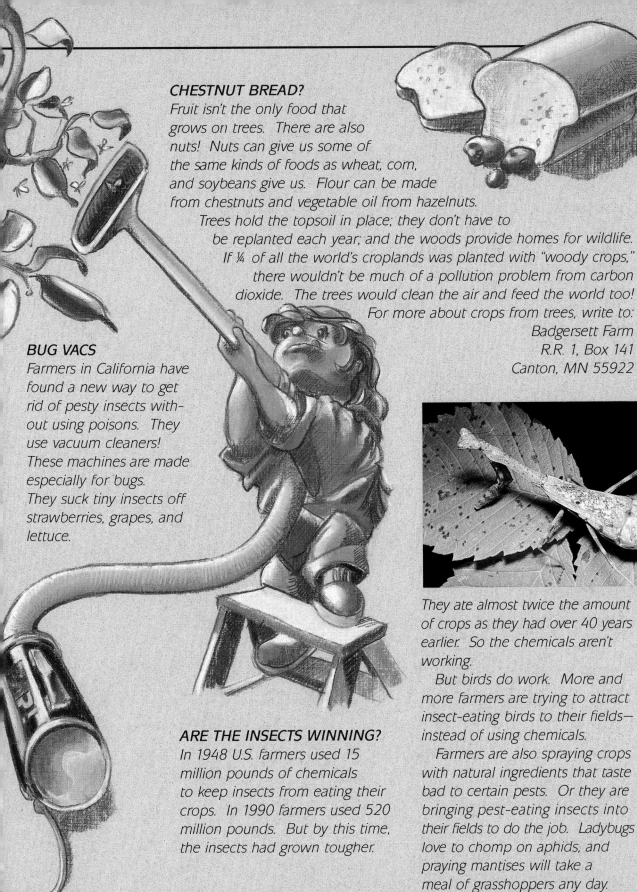

CHESTNUT BREAD?

Fruit isn't the only food that grows on trees. There are also nuts! Nuts can give us some of the same kinds of foods as wheat, corn, and soybeans give us. Flour can be made from chestnuts and vegetable oil from hazelnuts.

Trees hold the topsoil in place; they don't have to be replanted each year; and the woods provide homes for wildlife. If ¼ of all the world's croplands was planted with "woody crops," there wouldn't be much of a pollution problem from carbon dioxide. The trees would clean the air and feed the world too! For more about crops from trees, write to:

Badgersett Farm
R.R. 1, Box 141
Canton, MN 55922

BUG VACS

Farmers in California have found a new way to get rid of pesty insects without using poisons. They use vacuum cleaners! These machines are made especially for bugs. They suck tiny insects off strawberries, grapes, and lettuce.

ARE THE INSECTS WINNING?

In 1948 U.S. farmers used 15 million pounds of chemicals to keep insects from eating their crops. In 1990 farmers used 520 million pounds. But by this time, the insects had grown tougher.

They ate almost twice the amount of crops as they had over 40 years earlier. So the chemicals aren't working.

But birds do work. More and more farmers are trying to attract insect-eating birds to their fields—instead of using chemicals.

Farmers are also spraying crops with natural ingredients that taste bad to certain pests. Or they are bringing pest-eating insects into their fields to do the job. Ladybugs love to chomp on aphids, and praying mantises will take a meal of grasshoppers any day.

Wildlife Adventures

Take a Hike

Across the country,
parks have been set up to
save wild animals and plants,
and their habitats.
These parks are great places
to see how wild species live.

Always remember, though, not to
come up close to wild animals.
They need space
just as people do.

BECOME A NATURE DETECTIVE

You can learn a lot about animals by studying the tracks they make and the droppings they leave. People who know the land can read signs like tracks, feathers, rubbings, and diggings. They can tell you what animals were in the area recently and what they were doing. Often they can tell you some of the history of a place too—when a fire happened, when there was a season of dry weather, or where a tree was clawed by a bear or rubbed on by a buck.

Some kids' groups, such as the Boy Scouts, the Girl Scouts and Girl Guides, the Campfire Boys and Girls, and 4-H, can teach you how to read signs in nature. Nature centers and books in the library can give you a good start too. But the best way to learn is to spend as much time as possible outdoors, quietly looking, listening, feeling, and smelling. Soon you'll become a regular Sherlock Holmes.

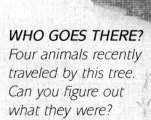

WHO GOES THERE?

Four animals recently traveled by this tree. Can you figure out what they were?

NIGHT SIGHT

Many animals come out at night, so how can you see them? Wrap a red piece of tissue paper, cellophane, or plastic around the bulb end of your flashlight. Then go outside with a friend or parent, and sit silently in one spot to watch and listen. Most night animals are not disturbed by red light.

A fluttering of wings and a screech may alert you to an owl's approach. A flash of a white tail whooshes by—was it a mouse? Two gleaming lights look at you—are you facing a raccoon? If they flit by, maybe they're fireflies. Who knows what you'll discover!

PLEASE DO NOT DISTURB!

Animals need time to rest too. Some animals are endangered because they spend so much energy during the day running away from people and their pets that they are too tired and hungry to get food for themselves and their young.

The piping plover is a little shorebird that lives on East Coast beaches in the summer. Since beaches are so popular, the plovers are constantly on the move, running to escape. People step on their nests in the sand, and dogs dig up their eggs. Picnickers leave food on the beach, and this attracts raccoon and foxes. These animals love to eat the plovers and their eggs. Some cities, counties, and parks are roping off sections of beach to give the piping plovers and other shore animals a place to live and nest in peace. So whenever you go into the great outdoors, do your best not to disturb the wildlife. They need all the energy they have to survive.

PUT THE WOODS IN A BOOK

How can you take the outdoors inside with you?

Bring a notebook with you. Write descriptions, draw pictures, add photographs, and press leaves in between the pages. Soon you'll have a record of all your nature experiences. If you note the time, date, and weather, you'll get to watch the seasons change when you read your book later.

Making a map of your favorite habitat can help you know it better. Think up names for all the nooks and crannies. Write down the kinds of plants found in each place. Mark the spots where you've seen nests and burrows.

Weeds or Wildflowers?

Every plant has a purpose
and a place.
The plant you call a weed
may be putting important
vitamins or minerals into the soil.
Or the weed's flowers and seeds
may be food for wild animals.
The weed could be a
wildflower that's attracting
bees and butterflies,
which help the plants near
the weed grow fruits and nuts.

Or perhaps it's even a plant
from a different country
that's out of its habitat,
such as a dandelion.
Dandelions came from Europe.
So what's a weed?
It's simply a plant out of place,
or one whose job hasn't
been noticed yet.

WILD AND WINDY CITY

One of the biggest cities
in the U.S. is named after a
wildflower—the wild onion. This
plant grows in the Midwest, and
the Winnebago Indians call it
Shi-ka-go. Chicago!

WILDFLOWER WISDOM

Watch the roadsides,
ditches, or vacant lots
around your home. In most
seasons, you'll see plants
blooming. These are
wildflowers. Birds eat
their seeds, bees drink
their nectar, spiders spin
webs around their blades,
rabbits hide among their
stalks, and deer eat their
leaves.

Find a guidebook in the
library on the wildflowers
native to your area, and
become a plant scout.
Sketch the leaves and
flowers, and learn how
to identify them. (Avoid
collecting the plants or
picking rare wildflowers.

Sometimes it takes years
for a plant to make one
flower.) In no time at all,
you'll find something
exciting in every crack in
the sidewalk, every vacant
lot, every dirt trail.

For information on
growing your own native
wildflowers, write to:
Clearinghouse
National Wildflower
Research Center
2600 FM 973 North
Austin, TX 78725-4201

If you can find a magnifying glass, you'll get an even closer view. Check out guidebooks from the library to identify the animals and plants you're seeing. You'll probably end up making a few new friends.

Some of these friends have no backbones, such as butterflies and snails, and they are having trouble finding habitats. Members of the Xerces Society work to protect them. To find out how to become a member, write to them at:

10 Southwest Ash St.
Portland, OR 92704

GET A GRASSHOPPER'S VIEW

Bend down to look at plants, and you've entered a mini-habitat. Take a look at the caterpillar crawling up a stalk, the moth flitting from flower to flower, the spiders catching flies in its web, the mushrooms, lichen, garter snakes, and snails. There's a whole world to explore here. Sit and watch how every creature goes about its business. What business is it? Can you tell?

PLANT AND ANIMAL BULLIES

If plants and animals are moved from their natural habitats to new places, they can become a problem. In their new homes, there are often no animals, insects, or diseases to eat them, and their numbers grow too quickly. They push out other plants and animals.

A bully plant in North America is the Eurasian milfoil. It was brought over to the U.S. to be put in tropical fish tanks. But some people dumped their tanks and milfoil into lakes. The plant grows so fast that it soon covered the tops of lakes and smothered them. When people took their boats from invaded lakes to clean lakes, they spread the milfoil. Killer bees, starlings, English house sparrows, fire ants, gypsy moths, water hyacinths, Asian mosquitoes, Asian cockroaches, zebra mussels, and purple loosestrife are all bullies in North America. Scientists have to work hard to find ways to control these bullies without hurting native species. So when you travel, be careful what you take from one place to another. (It's against the law to bring in plants and insects from other countries.)

Calling All Birds

Birds come in all
shapes, sizes, and colors,
and with all different songs.
Yet, because birds often
must hide to stay alive,
they aren't always easy to see.
That's what makes bird-watching
fun—it's a real challenge.
Watch for birds in parks,
on power lines, in ditches,
on fenceposts, in marshes,
and on rooftops.
Binoculars can help you see them.
Keep a notebook of all
the birds you've spotted.
Draw their pictures or
describe what
they look like.

Borrow a field guide
from the library
to find out their names.
Write down where and when
you saw them.
That way you'll get to know
their habits and
where they like to roost.
If you listen carefully,
you'll even learn their songs.

FOOD FOR FOWL

People like to feed bread to ducks, geese, and swans. But it can harm the birds. It weighs birds down and makes it harder for them to fly on long trips. So if you want to feed waterfowl, ask the nature center in your area what the best food is.

BIRDERS' BINGO

Parks in big cities are wonderful places to see birds, especially during the spring and summer. Migrating birds use these parks to rest and eat up.

You can make a contest with your friends and family. Keep a tally of all the different species you have seen. Who can spot the shy birds? Who can see the most birds in one morning? One afternoon? Sunrise is a great time to see birds. (The early birder gets the bird!) Sunsets are also good. Why not try a bird-watching walk before dinner?

BIRDS FOR ALL SEASONS

The Audubon Society loves birds. Call your local group, and see if you and your family or friends can go with them on a field trip. If you ask, they might even teach you about bird banding and feather marking. These are good ways to learn about how birds act and how far they travel. For more information on these methods of studying birds, write to:

Bird Banding Laboratory
Office of Migratory
Bird Management
Laurel, MD 20708

TREATS FOR ALL TASTES

Fill your feeders with treats for different kinds of birds. What do finches, grosbeaks, and buntings like? SEEDS, especially sunflower and thistle seeds. What will thrushes devour? FRUITS, such as raisins. (Baltimore orioles go crazy over orange slices!) What attracts the insect eaters—the woodpeckers, wrens, and warblers? SUET, made of animal fat, seeds, and chopped nuts.

(Cleaning your feeders regularly will help keep your visitors healthy.)

BIRD FEASTS

One way to see birds is to get them to come visit you. Plant wildflowers and sunflowers in your yard or on your balcony. Birds will fly in to drink the nectar, eat the seeds, or even eat the insects on the plants.

Or hang a glass jar sideways from a tree. Take off the lid and fill it with seeds. This will keep your birds fat even when snow covers the ground. A pinecone dipped in honey works too. (Don't use peanut butter, because birds can choke on it.) You can also plant trees and bushes with late-fall fruit, such as American Mountain Ash and bittersweet. The fruit hangs on the branches throughout winter.

At the Watering Hole

Whether you live next
to an ocean, a river,
a lake, a pond, a swamp,
or even a puddle,
there's a lot of life
to watch: minnows
and mosquitoes,
clams and crayfish,
sea gulls and snakes,
manatees and mice,
otters and alligators.
Any place near water
is a great place to watch wildlife.
Get to know the watering
holes in your area.
Then visit an aquarium
to learn about the creatures
under the water.

HABITS AT THE HABITAT

Animals get into daily habits too. Visit the nearest body of water at different times of the day. Keep track of which birds come at what time. Watch what they eat. When are the bugs the most active? When do fish gather in the shallow water? Where do the turtles like to hang out?

If you take notes on everything you see, pretty soon you'll know the habits of all the creatures at the watering hole just like you know the habits of your family.

LOVE THOSE LIZARDS!

Q: What's the closest thing to a dinosaur you can find?
A: A lizard. In fact, dinosaur means "terrible lizard." There are almost 3,000 species of lizards, and some live near you. So go out and see what little dinosaurs you can find.

Salamanders are called "spring lizards," but they're not really lizards at all. Yet they're regular visitors to many watering holes, and they're a lot of fun to watch.

MOTORBOAT, MOTORBOAT, GO SO FAST

Some people call motorboats "stinkpots," because their gas pollutes the air and water. These folks think it's more fun to row a boat, paddle a canoe, sail a sailboat, or travel in a rubber raft. These activities are quiet, so it's easy to approach a family of ducklings, slide past some feeding deer, or glide silently through a patch of water lilies. Plus, rowing, paddling, and sailing build muscles, and they don't pollute.

THE PLASTIC PROBLEM

Many scientists believe that plastic trash kills as many seals and other ocean wildlife as oil spills do. Anything left on a beach can be dangerous. Shorebirds, otters, beavers, ducks, seals, and fish get tangled in old fishing line and nets. They choke on balloon bits. They get caught around the neck by plastic rings from canned drinks. That's why it's important to leave a beach or other habitat cleaner than how you found it. It's also a good idea to avoid buying canned drinks with plastic rings—or to cut the rings before you toss them in the garbage. Can you think of other ways to help solve the plastic problem?

HOOTS, HOWLS, AND HONKS

Animals communicate with their own sounds and language. Many times you can attract animals by learning their calls and imitating them. Can you honk like a Canada goose? Or hoot like an owl? Croak like a bullfrog? Sing like a wren?

Some people can imitate wildlife sounds so well that the animals and birds call back. People howling at wolves hear them howl in reply. Many birders whistle or use bird-calling tapes to attract the birds they want to see.

The more you listen to wildlife calls, the more you'll hear how they use some calls for mating, some for alarm, and some for just chatting. You don't need to be Dr. Doolittle to understand and talk to the animals!

Nature's Students

As we have seen, the world of nature is exciting and complex. Everything is related to everything else. Even *we* are a part of nature.

Many environmental schools and nature centers offer programs for school groups, clubs, kids, families, and teachers to explore everything from wolves to wetlands. Some offer summer camps and wilderness experiences too. Here's a sampling of places you can write to for more information.

Kiwanis Camp Wyman
600 Kiwanis Drive
Eureka, MO 63025

National Arbor Day
  Foundation
Discovery Camp
100 Arbor Avenue
Nebraska City, NE 68410

CANADA
Federation of
  Ontario Naturalists
355 Less Mill Road
Dawn Mills, Ontario
  M3B 2W8

Wind Cave National Park
R.R. 1, Box 190-WCNP
Hot Springs, SD 57747

MIDWEST
Ebersole Environmental
  Education Center
3400 Second Street
Wayland, MI 49348

Wolf Ridge
  Environmental Center
230 Cranberry Road
Finland, MN 55603

Edudex Associates
Kettle Moraine Div.
604 2nd Avenue
West Bend, WI 53095

NORTHEAST
Adirondack Outdoor
  Education Center
Camp Chingachgook
on Lake George
Kattskill Bay, NY 12844

Appalachian Mountain Club
Pinkham Notch Visitor Center
P.O. Box 298BZ
Gorham, NH 03581

Audubon Naturalist Society
Central Atlantic States
8940 Jones Mill Road
Chevy Chase, MD 20815

Betsy-Jeff Penn 4-H
  Educational Center
R.R. 13, Box 249X
Reidsville, NC 27320

Brooklyn Center for the
  Urban Environment
Tennis House
Prospect Park
Brooklyn, NY 11215-9992

Brookside Nature Center
1400 Glenallen Avenue
Wheaton, MD 20902

Chewonki Foundation
R.R.2, Box 1200
Wiscasset, ME 04578

Journey's End Farm Camp
RR 1, Box 136
Newfoundland, PA 18455

Keewaydin Environmental
   Education Center
Lake Dunmore
Salisbury, VT 05769

NWF Wildlife Camps
1400 16th Street NW
Washington, DC 20036

Pocono Environmental
   Education Center
R.D. 2, Box 1010
Dingmans Ferry, PA 18328

Riverbend Environmental
   Education Center
P.O. Box 2
Gladwyne, PA 19035

PACIFIC NORTHWEST
Island Institute
4004 58th Place S.W.
Seattle, WA 98116

North Cascades Institute
2105 Highway 20
Sedro Woolley, WA 98284

Trailside Discovery
4325 Laurel Street
Suite 240
Anchorage, AK 99508

SOUTHEAST
Chattanooga Nature Center
400 Garden Road
Chattanooga, TN 37419

Museum of Science
   and Industry
4801 East Fowler Avenue
Tampa, FL 33617

Newfound Harbor
   Marine Institute
Route 3, Box 170
Big Pine Key, FL 33043

SOUTHWEST
Camp Allen
   Discovery Program
R.R. 1, Box 426
Navasota, TX 77868

Treetops-in-the-Forest
809 East Coral Way
Grand Prairie, TX 75051

WEST
Catalina Island
   Marine Institute
   Guided Discoveries
P.O. 1360
Claremont, CA 91711

Estes Park Center
YMCA of the Rockies
2515 Tunnel Road
Estes Park, CO 80511

Four Corners School
   of Outdoor Ed.
Dept. BZ, East Route
Monticello, UT 84535

Keystone Science School
Box 8606
Keystone, CO 80435

NWF Western Wildlife Camp
1400 16th Street NW
Washington, DC 20036

San Francisco Bay
   National Wildlife Refuge
P.O. 524
Newark, CA 94560

Teton Science School
P.O. Box 68
Kelly, WY 83011

Three Circles Center
   for Multi-Cultural
   Environmental Ed.
P.O. 1946
Sausalito, CA 94965

Wolf's Creek Nature Camp
Office of Extended Ed.
Humboldt State University
Arcata, CA 95521

Where Do We Go from Here?

An Expert Opinion

We could spend our whole lives exploring the soil, air, water, plants, animals, and habitats, and still have many mysteries yet to solve. Here are some people who can help you find answers to some of your earthwise questions (ask your teachers how to reach them):

Audubon Society members
Bird-watchers
Botanists (people who study plants)
City council members
City planners
Conservationists (people who work to save habitats and species)
Conservation biologists
Entomologists (people who study insects)
Environmental lobbyists (people who work with lawmakers to make good laws for the earth)
Environmental clubs
Environmental planners
National and International Wildlife Federation members

Naturalists
Oceanographers (people who study oceans)
Ornithologists (people who study birds)
Park and forestry rangers
Restoration ecologists (people who work to bring an area back to its wild state)
Science teachers
Sierra Club members
Soil scientists
Sustainable farmers
Wilderness Society members
Wildlife specialists
Zookeepers
Zoologists (people who study animals)

You can also read *Earthwise at Home* and *Earthwise at School*.